THE ADVENTURES OF
JOBBY

Written by Dorothy Shepherd
Illustrated by Amy Curran

THE ADVENTURES OF JOBBY
ISBN: 978-0-6484496-4-5

Published in Australia by
PINK COFFEE PUBLISHING
PO Box 483, Oberon NSW 2787
www.pinkcoffeepublishing.com

Text Copyright Dorothy Shepherd 2020
Illustrations Copyright Amy Curran 2020
All Rights Reserved

National Library of Australia Cataloguing-in-Publication entry information can be found at www.nla.gov.au

CONTENTS

Chapter One	5
Chapter Two	10
Chapter Three	15
Chapter Four	20
Chapter Five	24
Chapter Six	26
Chapter Seven	29
Chapter Eight	32
Chapter Nine	35
Chapter Ten	37
Chapter Eleven	39
About The Author	41
About The Illustrator	42

CHAPTER 1
The Beginning

I was born on the eighth of October, 1994.

When I saw my mum and my brothers and sisters I felt such warmth.

For six weeks, I had lovely people around me.

One day, while I was playing with my sisters in the warm sun, I looked up and suddenly saw a lady standing beside my pen. She was carrying a large wicker basket and talking to the man who fed my mum.

The door opened and in they came. The feeder began to pick us up one by one and put us in the basket. I was terrified, but I did not want my sisters to see it. They were crying and howling.

The basket lid was closed firmly, and we were all alone without our mum. Thrust from the sunlight into the darkness. I heard Mum howling and I became scared. Somehow I knew I would never see her again.

The basket bumped down and I heard a terrifying sound. I now know it was just the car engine, but at that time we had never heard anything like it. We huddled together, a shaking mass.

Just as I thought the noise would go on for ever, it suddenly stopped. I felt the basket being lifted up, and then we were carried for a while and put down with another sharp bump. When someone raised the lid of the basket, I poked my head up and found that we were inside a building. It smelled strange, like other dogs but also scents I did not recognise. I was to discover later that this building was a pet shop.

We were all put into a box with straw in the bottom, and although I had my sisters with me, I felt lonely and lost. At least the lady who had brought us here fed us regularly. Not with the warm milk my mother had provided, though. It took us a long time to get used to the strange new food, it was very different to mothers milk.

Several days passed, and I began to get used to my new, strange surroundings. Other people came into the shop and played with us for a while but then they left through a big green door. I desperately wanted to know what the world beyond that door was like.

One day, a lady came into the shop and knelt on the floor and put her hand inside the cage. I had been sleeping on top of my sister, who got up as well, and I almost knocked her over as I rushed to the lady and started licking her hand.

I jumped up and down enthusiastically. I really like this person, I thought. I hope she likes me too. She stayed for a while, then she stood up and went over to the counter and talked to the man there. I saw her taking some money out of her purse, and giving it to the man behind the counter. Then she walked over to the cage, tickled my tummy… and left!

I was so sad. I had really hoped this lady would like me enough to take me home with her, because she seemed so kind. What I did not know was that I was in quarantine and could not leave the shop for two weeks.

Every day I studied the people in the shop, to see if I could recognise the kind lady again, but to no avail.

Then one day, the door of the shop opened, and in walked my lady! She had another lady with her. They came over to the cage, tickled me, and then went over to the shop counter.

I saw my lady opening her purse and taking out some money. Then the two ladies followed the pet shop man over to the cage and plucked me out of the melee. My sisters were crying and I was sorry to leave them behind… but I was a big boy now and I had a person who owned me!

CHAPTER 2
A New Life

One of the ladies carried me against her chest. I was a bit scared as there were lots of people rushing about the streets, and lots of cars. She got into a parked car, and this time I was put onto a seat instead of into the boot.

After a short journey, I was carried into a house. The kind lady (who I later knew as Jacquie, my owner's daughter), carried me into a large room and placed me on the knee of a man who was sitting on the chair.

"What is it?" he asked.

"A German Shepherd," said Jacquie.

Then everyone laughed, because I think they knew I was NOT a German Shepherd, but a sweet cuddly Jack Russell terrier. The man, who I now know as Louis, stroked me and I licked his fingers.

My owner, whose name was Dorothy, picked me up and deposited me in a comfortable new basket. I was so tired after all the new experiences that I fell soundly asleep. I slept for hours and hours.

When I awoke, I saw I had my own drinking bowl and also a food bowl beside my basket. Life was not going to be too bad at all...!

My legs were so short I could barely climb out of my basket the first time. But Dorothy helped me, and I was soon scampering in and out of it quite easily. I made noises at the back door, and Dorothy let me out into a large garden with flowers and plants everywhere.

One afternoon I was playing out in the garden, I heard some children laughing. I scurried over to them. They were three girls, who told me their names were Louise, Jessica and Melissa. They had come to visit for a holiday.

I looked up to the sky, and there was an enormous Christmas tree, with decorations and tinsel and a bright shining star on top.

I played with the girls for a long time, but the sun was hot and I was small and I needed my rest. I fell asleep under the Christmas tree.

During the holidays I met a man called Nigel, too, and his little son AJ. They lived near us and I visited them lots of times, even after the holidays were over, running around in their big garden. I had to watch out for AJ. Because he was small, he sometimes stepped on my toes.

This idyllic life continued for a few weeks until, one morning, I heard the girls chattering and saw Jacquie loading suitcases into the car. Their holiday was over and they were returning home. I was going to miss them.

I could tell Dorothy and Louis were upset too. Dogs can feel these things.

Later that day, Dorothy had to go to work, and I stayed home with Louis. Both of us felt very miserable.

CHAPTER 3
Training My People

Life went on, and I was growing daily.

The long summer days were filled with joy. Lots of things to do, lots of places to explore.

I had a new friend, too. His name was Odo, and he belonged to Nigel's family. We loved to run and tumble together in Nigel's garden.

One thing I hated though, was having a bath!

If I saw Dorothy running the taps in the laundry, I took off down the garden. I usually got caught, but I hated my fur being sodden. Luckily it did not happen too often!

One morning I awoke and went into the garden for my morning patrol. I had to check every day that no cats were hiding in the bushes!

Dorothy was at work and Louis was getting into a strange car. I heard them say it was a hire car.

Louis was away for hours, and when he returned he brought some strangers into the house. I heard them say they had travelled all the way from England. These people were called visitors.

These "visitors" were the dearest people. I loved them from the start. They played with me, and the one called Les took me for walks on my leash. I noticed they made my people laugh a lot!

We had trips out in the car, in the hot summer weather, and lots of long walks in the garden.

However, the day came when they too carried their suitcases out to their car and left us.

There was another time I remember while on my morning patrol, a beautiful sunny morning. I saw Dorothy putting clothes into suitcases, and I thought we must be going on a trip together!

I felt very excited!

We jumped into the car and started to drive, I was eagerly watching the scenary as we went.

We reached a driveway with large gates, that I later learned were called "the kennels".

I stayed there for two weeks, and I was very sad and miserable without my people.

There were dogs everywhere, and we had only two walks every day in the field, and nothing to do in between except BARK.

I hated it, and worried my people might never come back for me.

One day, the kennel man put on my leash, and led me to the front office. There was Dorothy.

I was ecstatic! I jumped up and down and spun around in circles! My people had not forgotten me!

They took me home and I explored everywhere, checking that all my toys were still there in the right places. That night I went to sleep in my own basket, I was a very happy dog!

CHAPTER 4
My Interstate Trip

Things quickly got back to normal and continued that way for a few weeks until, once again, I saw Dorothy had those dreaded suitcases out in the bedroom, and, once again she was putting clothes into them.

I decided that, come what may, I would never go back to those terrible kennels. I decided to guard the cases, and every time Dorothy went into the bedroom, there I was!

But this time she did not put the cases into the car. I could not understand what was happening.

In the morning, we got up really early and they put me in the car, with all my toys and my bed. We drove for hours, and when we stopped, another person met us. His name was Neil. I decided I liked him a lot. He patted me and made a big fuss of me, then he carried me out into his car with all my belongings… and drove off and left my people standing there waving goodbye!

I was not sure why we were driving away from my people, I thought maybe they could have been going on one of those 'holidays' that people went on, like when the children came to stay with us. I hoped I would see them again.

We had another long drive, to Neil's place, where I met Gill and Ellie. Ellie was the Border Collie that lived there, and she licked everyone a lot!

It was soon night and Neil put my bed in the garage beside Ellie's and left us to sleep. I had never slept outside a house before, and Ellie was licking me all over and my people had abandoned me, so I howled, and whined and howled some more.

At twelve o'clock, Neil came out of the house, took my bed and put it in the laundry room. Things were looking up! I settled down to sleep in the new room, thinking that things were not going to be too bad after all.

I stayed with Neil and Gill for a few months. One day when Ellie was teaching me how to eat grass, and I was teaching her how to chew clothes pegs, I heard a familiar sound. It was MY PEOPLE'S CAR! I went crazy. They were back! They loved me, they had not forgotten me! I danced and skipped and licked and jumped all over them.

The next day, we all got in the car. I gave a big thank-you lick to both Neil and Gill, barked goodbye to Ellie, and we all drove home.

It was a very long drive, but it was worth it to see my garden, my house and all my toys again.

HOME! HOME!

CHAPTER 5
Baths and Brushes

After we returned home from Neil and Gills house in Canberra, we spent the rest of the winter tidying the gardens at Somerville and Crib Point.

When I went to Crib Point, Odo and I spent most of our time tearing around the back garden, getting in everyone's feet! It was rather muddy after all the winter rains, and I am sorry to say we both got into rather a muddy state. Odo was worse than I, because he is a Shitszu/Maltese terrier cross, and he had a lovely long white coat. You can imagine the mess that he got that coat into. So much so, that Nigel had to clip it all off! He made him look like a lion! He had a mane at the front and short hair at the back. I had to giggle when I saw him for the first time. Odo was really annoyed with me, when he saw me doing this. But, I was not too happy for long, as we I got home, I was firmly put into the laundry trough and BATHED!

It was still quite cold, but not as cold as it had been in Canberra. I had grown my own coat especially for the cold winds in Canberra, when I was holidaying there. When I got back to Victoria, I began to shed it. Consequently my hair was all over the place. It was in the house, all over my bed and all over the car.

Soon, I discovered something else I HATED! It was called a dog brush! Dorothy made me sit, and then she brushed me with this brush. It was spiky and I did not like it at all, so I pretended NOT to hear her when she called me, especially when I could see that dreaded brush in her hand. I had to get used to it though as it became a daily routine, and I did get a dog chocolate drop when she had finished, so maybe it wasn't all bad.

CHAPTER 6
Birthday Parties

Then, came AJ's birthday. I heard my people say that AJ would soon be two years old and we were going to his birthday party which was to be held at a Fish and Chip shop in Melbourne. They all talked of birthday cakes and presents, and then I heard them say that Postman Pat would be there, and his black and white CAT!

I could not wait for the day to arrive, when I could chase that black and white cat all over the restaurant! I was very excited as the day approached, I thought Odo and I could really give it a good scare!

Everyone got ready to go in the car, and horrors.................. they were not taking me.

They left me in the laundry by myself, telling me to be a GOOD BOY!

I had a cushion in there to curl up on, but, I was so mad! While they were away, I tore the cushion into thousands of tiny pieces.

There was stuffing everywhere. Up my nose, in my ears, and in my mouth, but mostly all OVER the floor.

I stood back exhausted. Then I heard the key opening the door. I looked at the mess, and I felt very ashamed, so I hid under the towel I had pulled down onto the floor.

Voices sounded loudly... "Naughty boy!", "Who did this?" I kept myself hidden under the safety of the towel.

The stuffing was gradually cleaned up. Only then did I think it was safe to come out of my hiding place. Wagging my tail, slowly at first, and then gradually faster and faster, I approached them. It was a great ploy!

After many more stern warnings like "do NOT do anything like this again" they eventually forgave me and gave me a piece of birthday cake. It was delicious!

CHAPTER 7
Off we go again

One morning in October, my people began packing things into the car again. This time I was going with them. I was determined! We drove for hours and hours, and finally arrived in Canberra. I knew it was Canberra, because I stuck my nose out of the window and I could smell Canberra smells. Horses, mountains and other smells.

We passed the lake and Parliament House and then down through the tunnel. Finally, we drove into Neil and Gill's driveway. I could not wait to get out, I was twitching and squirming on Dorothy's knee. Soon I would see my friend Ellie again.

The front door opened and there was Neil. I jumped out of the car and made a big fuss of him.

I licked him, jumped up to his knees and he bent down and stroked me. Dorothy took me through the house into the back garden. I was just about to rush out to find Ellie, when I smelt another dog smell. The hackles stood up on the back of my neck. There was another dog in Ellie's and my garden!

I looked up as this strange dog bounded up to me and tried to put his foot on my back. The dog was white with black spots and I heard Neil call him Harley! I growled and growled, but he did not appear to take any notice of me.

So I gave him a good nip on his leg, especially as he was trying to get a pat from Dorothy and Louis. I still had not said "hello" to Ellie. I went back inside the house and sat down quietly watching the door in case this strange dog tried to get inside.

Well readers, I spent a miserable two days with Harley, the Dalmatian. He was even allowed to sleep in the lounge room, while I had to sleep in the laundry and poor Ellie was sleeping in the garage!

I thought I was going to have to stay with him, while my people went off again. Then, I heard them say to Neil, it may be better if I came with them to Jacquie's place.

I was relieved. Anything, would be better than staying there with that Harley dog!

CHAPTER 8
NSW or Bust!

We had another long drive to New South Wales and finally arrived in Pelaw Main. I had not been there before and as I stuck my nose out of the window I could smell lots of new odours.

I jumped out of the car and horrors, to my dismay I could see two large German Shepherd dogs in the back yard! Talk about "out of the frying pan into the fire". What had I done?

Then I saw the girls, whom I had last seen my first Christmas. Louise, Jessica and Melissa. I licked them all over and jumped up at them so they would know how very pleased I was to see them again.

I suddenly had a thought, perhaps, if I pretended to be a German Shepherd too, those dogs would not tear me limb from limb!

Everytime I went outside into the front yard, I ran up to the fence where the dogs (Bill and Ben were their names) were contained, and barked furiously at them. I could see I was scaring them both, by the surprised look on their faces!

Everyone morning and evening I took the girls for a walk in the park. I allowed them to hold my leash. Sometimes we walked to the school with Louise and Jessica. There were another two large dogs on the way there, and also two horses in a field. I was not upset by these, as I knew they could not get out at me.

It was a very happy time for me, and I realised I was the only dog allowed in the house. Bill and Ben got as far as the back verandah and I could look at them out of the window. I think they were really scared of me by now!

Louise thought I would bite her with my sharp white teeth. I never would though, I just like to nibble her fingers! I am proud of my teeth I keep them sharp and white by eating my bones.

The days were warm. The walks were good. One day we were walking in the park, when we thought we could see a snake! I was just about to tear its head off, when Dorothy said it was only a dead lizard! Louise decided we should go home just in case a snake came out to investigate it!

All good things come to an end, and before long we were packing up the car ready for another journey. I hoped we were not driving all the way home in one go, as I find it a very boring journey. I had managed to cover all the car in my dog hair, and it was starting to look very untidy!

CHAPTER 9
Nowra here we come

I heard my people say we were stopping off in Nowra to see Clive. We drove for a couple of hours and then began a terrifying journey down some very big mountains and into a valley.

Finally, we came to a town and pulled up outside a house. Dorothy got out of the car. She went up to a man standing on the driveway and gave him a big hug!

Louis and I got out of the car and put me on my leash. I understood why, when I saw another German Shepherd standing in the garage. He was looking at me with a quizzical look. So I ran up to him and gave him a nip on his leg. He looked very surprised! And stood with his mouth open. I heard Clive say "stay Cujo" so now I knew his name.

I was allowed to go into the house for a drink of water and everyone else sat down and had a cup of coffee. We climbed back into the car and did that horrible journey up the hills again and drove for a little while longer and finally arrived at Neil and Gill's place. That dreaded Harley was still there!

Having lived through three experiences with German Shepherds, I was now a tiger. Nothing frightened me. So, for the next few days I chased Harley all around the garden. Ellie looked on in disgust.

CHAPTER 10
Home again

Well, it was that time again. A time to travel home. We arrived back tired but happy. Especially me, I had met lots of new friends and caught up with old ones too. I settled down to my duties of chasing cats and birds out of my garden.

Soon, it was summer. Odo's coat had grown again and he had stopped looking like a lion. We played a lot in the garden while everyone was busy building gates and things at Crib Point.

We had a lot of visitors. Two girls came to see me, Tracie and Leanne. They played with me, and threw the ball for me to play with. Louis' friends Derek and Blanche came to show us their new four wheel drive car.

One week in summer, Neil and Gill arrived to visit. Guess what - they brought the Harley dog with them. I told him "this is my pad my friend. No sleeping in the lounge. You can sleep in the laundry. Guess what - he did!

The day Neil and Gill were leaving, I found Harley in the back garden and he was all yellow! I knew he would be in trouble. He had been digging in Louis' sand pile! I hid in the bushes until Neil and Louis came back. When Neil saw him and the mess he had made, he went crazy. I had to have a laugh, as usually it was me that got into trouble!

The last I saw of Harley, was him being put into the car, still a really nice yellow colour. "Goodbye Harley", I yelped! He looked very sorry as he was driven away.

CHAPTER 11
Christmas

Soon it was Christmas once more, and we started to prepare everything. The outside Christmas Tree was decorated and we also bought one for outside the front door. We covered this tree in bells and baubles with tinsel and we placed an angel on the top. It looked splendid.

Christmas morning we had Kevin, Kerry and Lora as well as Nigel, Desiree and AJ all opening presents at the same time.

I too, had a Christmas stocking, which I managed to open all by myself. Santa had brought me a Bananas in Pyjamas doll, a teddy and a squeaky bread roll.

Odo only got a squeaky ball, and this I had bought for him, knowing I could borrow it when I visited Crib Point.

We all had a splendid time and soon it was time for all the visitors to go home. I settled down with a full tummy of turkey and I had some really bad nightmares. I think I had eaten too much food.

The year had gone full circle. I had been with my people for one whole year. It is a good life and I have had some great adventures.

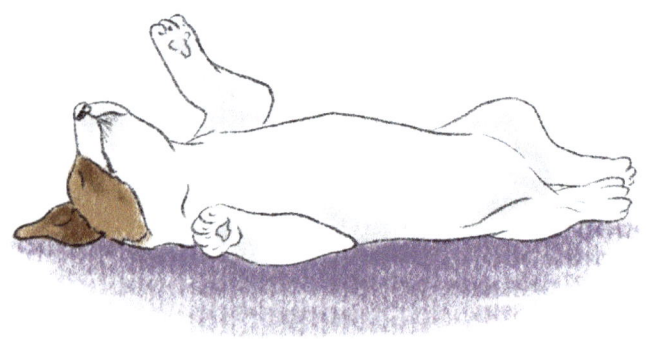

ABOUT THE AUTHOR

Dorothy Shepherd was born in Whitehaven in Cumberland, England, and in 1979 migrated to Australia. Dorothy wrote this book about her beloved dog Jobby, for the entertainment of her grandchildren and great grandchildren.

Dorothy lives on a property close to the Tarago village, in New South Wales, Australia, with her loving husband Louis.

Dorothy finished writing this book in 1996. As a gift for her 80th birthday, her children and their partners organised the book to come to life in printed form.

ABOUT THE ILLUSTRATOR

Amy Curran lives in the picturesque Blue Mountains area of New South Wales, Australia, with her four children and husband Scott.

Amy gained her Diploma in Children's Book Illustration with a Distinction from the London Art College.

The Adventures of Jobby by Dorothy Shepherd, is the 11th book that Amy has illustrated since gaining her Diploma.

www.amycurran.com.au

www.ingramcontent.com/pod-product-compliance
Lightning Source LLC
Chambersburg PA
CBHW051540010526
44107CB00064B/2800